This book is dedicated to my mother, Vonnie Snyder, who always believed that I could get this book published.

I also thank my husband, Martin, for being my "publication manager" through this whole process.

Table of Contents

Chapter 1 A Little Blond Puppy   3

Chapter 2 A Family   5

Chapter 3 Too Quiet   9

Chapter 4 Too Many Pets   11

Chapter 5 Too Lonely   15

Chapter 6 Molly Finds Her Family   19

Chapter 1

A Little Blond Puppy

The little blond puppy was looking for a family.

Yesterday she had been playing with her brothers and sisters. They had chased balls and climbed on top of each other. Their mother had fed them and kept them clean. The people in the house had come out to play with her. The puppy was happy.

But then she discovered a hole in the fence. Where did it go? What was on the other side? So, she squeezed through the hole and started to explore.

After a while, she had no idea which way to go to find her family. What should she do? The puppy missed her brothers and sisters.

When she saw some children playing together, she missed her brothers and sisters even more. She needed to play with someone, too.

So the blond puppy took off down the road. There must be a good home for her somewhere. There must be a home with plenty of food and a nice place to sleep. Surely there were children or other puppies that wanted to play with her.

But where?

Chapter 2

A Family

Around the corner, the puppy saw a boy pulling a wagon across his yard. The puppy ran up to the boy and looked in the wagon. There were all kinds of wonderful things in there. She saw two blue trucks, three yellow balls and a green dinosaur.

The little boy picked her up and put her in his wagon. He started pulling her around the yard. He stroked her fur. "You are such a cute dog," he said. Then he took her to meet his mom, dad and sister. Everyone wanted to hold her. The puppy liked that because it reminded her of her mother.

The family gave the puppy some yummy food. They gave her a rug to sleep on in the kitchen. They played with her every day. The dad built a great doghouse in the back yard. Mostly, she liked playing with the boy called Joshua.

They even gave her a name. They called her Molly.

Maybe this could be her new family. She had everything she wanted. She had lots of bones and leftover people food to eat. She had a nice bed inside the house and a great doghouse outside. She had fun playing catch-the-ball with Joshua and his sister, Rachel. Molly stayed with the family for several days.

But then she wondered. "Is there a better place? Is there something greater on the other side of the fence?" Molly just had to find out.

So, she looked for a way out of the back yard. She ran all around the edge of the fence. Then she found a place where the fence did not meet the ground. She pushed her way through the hole and slipped out.

"I wonder what else I can find," she thought as she took off down the street.

Chapter 3

Too Quiet

Soon Molly found an old man raking leaves. He stopped to pet her and scratch behind her ears. He called his wife to come and see the puppy he had found.

The old lady ran out of the house with bread for the puppy. They gave her some water. They picked her up and told her how cute she was. Molly loved getting all this attention.

The puppy decided to stay with the old couple. They gave her a warm bed in a basket and plenty of dog food. The puppy felt good in this house. Maybe this was her family.

But after a few days, Molly got tired of lying around and watching TV. She wanted to run and play. She missed having someone to throw a ball for her. She wanted someone to run across a field with her. She was bored.

The puppy tried to get the old man to play. But he just wanted to pet her and give her dog treats. He didn't want to run around. He didn't want to roll on the ground. And he didn't like to get licked at all!!

One day the puppy sat in the yard. She watched the man working in his garden. She wondered if there could be a better home down the street. The puppy had to find out. She quietly slipped away from the old man.

"I wonder what else I can find," Molly thought as she took off down the street.

Chapter 4

Too Many Pets

Later that day, the puppy saw two people riding bikes. She followed them. They stopped in the neighborhood park for a rest. She ran to them and wagged her tail as hard as she could. She wanted them to know how much she liked to run and play. The man looked at her and laughed.

"Do you want to play?" he asked. Molly jumped and ran in circles. The man and his wife threw a plastic disc for the puppy. She ran after it. She did not understand that she was supposed to bring it back. The man got the plastic disc and threw it again.

After a while, the puppy saw that she was supposed to bring the plastic disc back to the man. What a fun game!

When the man and his wife got back on their bikes, the little blond puppy followed them. She loved running along as they pedaled all the way home.

"This is a very cute dog," said the wife. "Let's give her something to eat."

The people had a cozy and warm house. They gave her a big soft pillow for her bed. They liked to play with her. And they gave her good things to eat. Molly felt good in this house. Maybe this was her family.

A few days later, the man brought home a pet parakeet. At first the parakeet stayed in her cage. But after a while, the man and his wife let the parakeet out of her cage. The bird flew around the house. The puppy got very worried. The bird dived down and nipped at Molly's floppy ears.

The young couple laughed at this. Molly tried to hide.

The puppy wondered if there could be a better home for her someplace else.

The next day she was outside running with the man and his wife. Molly just kept running and didn't come back.

"I wonder what else I can find," she thought as she took off down the road.

Chapter 5

Too Lonely

Molly was sniffing around in the bushes. She was hungry. When she looked up, she saw a pretty lady pushing a baby in a stroller. Molly had never seen such a thing before. She followed them home.

The lady spoke kindly to her and stopped to pet her. The baby laughed when she saw the puppy. The puppy wondered if this might be a good family for her.

At her house, the pretty lady gave the puppy water and a hot dog to eat. She even had a nice doghouse waiting in the back yard for Molly. She put some towels and an old pillow in the doghouse. The puppy crawled into the doghouse and took a long nap.

When the lady's husband came home, he went outside and played with Molly. He threw the ball. This time Molly knew to bring it back to him right away. They had a good time playing in the back yard. The puppy liked this place. Maybe this was the family for her.

When the man went back into the house, the puppy tried to follow him inside. The lady stopped them both at the door.

"No, no, no! Puppy, you can't come inside the house. " she said. "We have a baby in here. You might hurt her. Stay outside."

The puppy didn't understand. But she knew the lady did not want her inside. Molly was very lonely outside all night long.

The next day, no one came to play with her. In fact, no one seemed to be at home. Where did they go? When it was almost dark, they came back. But only the man came outside to feed her and play with her a little bit.

As the days went by, they hardly played with Molly at all.

Molly was very lonely. She wondered if there could be a better home someplace else.

"I wonder what else I can find." Once again, the little blond puppy found a place in the fence where she could slip out. She squeezed out of the back yard and took off down the road.

Chapter 6

Molly Finds Her Family

The little blond puppy stopped to rest in a small park. As she watched the children play, she thought of the family that called her Molly. She thought of Joshua and Rachel and their nice home. She thought about how Joshua's family had everything she was looking for.

They had given her good food. They had played with her every day. They had let her come in the house. They didn't have any other pets. And they had a great back yard. What more could she want?

Molly decided to go back to Joshua, Rachel, Mom and Dad. This would be her family. She had to think really hard to remember where their house was. She put her nose to the ground and started sniffing. She went back to all the places she had been in the last few days.

Molly passed by the house where the pretty lady and her husband and the baby lived. It didn't look like anyone was home. Molly kept sniffing the ground trying to find Joshua.

Molly ran very quickly by the house where the pet parakeet lived. She did not want to get anywhere near that bird. She wanted to be with Joshua.

The puppy crept by the house where the old couple lived. She did not want to go back in that house. It was too quiet in there! Joshua's house was a lot more fun.

Finally, she saw the house for which she was looking. Joshua's blue trucks, yellow balls and the green dinosaur were sitting in the wagon by the garage.

Molly ran up to the front door. She barked and scratched at the screen door.

Joshua shouted for joy when he saw Molly sitting on the front porch. He opened the door and Molly walked right in. Joshua called to the rest of the family, "Come, see who is at the front door."

"Yes!" Molly thought. "This is where I belong. This is my family. Everything is perfect here. I don't have to wonder anymore if there is a better home for me someplace else."

The whole family came running into the living room. They hugged Molly and told her how happy they were to see her.

"Where did you go, Molly?" asked Joshua. "Don't you know this is your home?"

"I know now," barked Molly.

AuthorHouse™
1663 Liberty Drive
Bloomington, IN 47403
www.authorhouse.com
Phone: 833-262-8899

Because of the dynamic nature of the Internet, any web addresses or links contained in this book may have changed since publication and may no longer be valid. The views expressed in this work are solely those of the author and do not necessarily reflect the views of the publisher, and the publisher hereby disclaims any responsibility for them.

Any people depicted in stock imagery provided by Getty Images are models, and such images are being used for illustrative purposes only.
Certain stock imagery © Getty Images.

This book is printed on acid-free paper.

ISBN: 978-1-4772-0370-5 (sc)
ISBN: 978-1-4772-0371-2 (e)

Library of Congress Control Number: 2012908039

Print information available on the last page.

Published by AuthorHouse 07/21/2023

authorHOUSE®

Printed in the United States
by Baker & Taylor Publisher Services